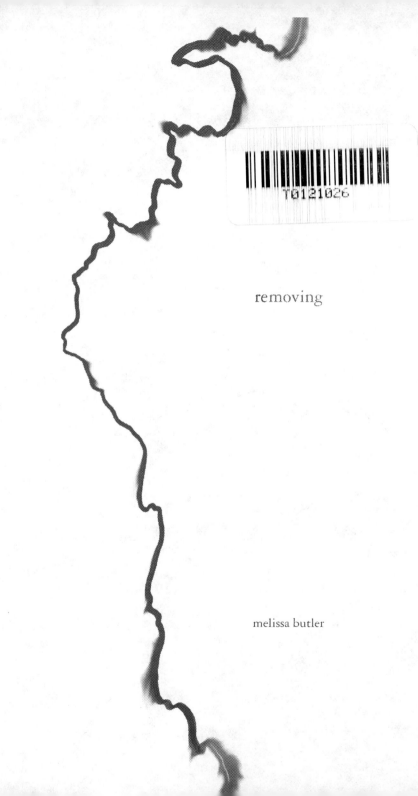

removing

melissa butler

'Cited' was previously published in *Carapace 67*.

Publication © Modjaji Books 2010

Text © Melissa Butler 2010

First published in 2010 by Modjaji Books

P O Box 385, Athlone, 7760, Cape Town, South Africa

http://modjaji.book.co.za

www.modjaji.book.co.za

ISBN 978-1-920397-19-7

Book and Cover design: Jacqui Stecher

Charcoal drawings: Jane Eppel

Cover photograph: Sarah Rohde

Printed by Megadigital

Set in Garamond 11/14

I *travel differently*

From the time I was young, I wanted to leave. My most vivid childhood memories are of watching people's feet from underneath a table. I took myself away from where I was and made up stories.

I have had 18 permanent addresses in my life. I have learned that permanence is always temporary. And my geographies are metaphysical. I have known home inside of moments: engaging in a community project, having a conversation across a table, watching a bird build a nest.

I came to South Africa from the U.S. for the first time in 2005. Originally, I came *here* in order to leave *there*. It was necessary to cross an ocean and live on this southern tip to realize that no matter where I go, I am still with myself. And perhaps this is why I have come to travel the way I do. I don't scatter myself across the earth's surface. I need the layers found in my return to a single place again and again.

I am drawn back to South Africa for many reasons: I study here, I work with schools in the Eastern Cape, I have good friends, I love the mountain, I need an outsider's distance in order to write. But there is nothing here to hold me other than my stories—no passport, no piece of land, no name anchored in the history of this place. My connection here is one of small commitments over time and something mixed from instinct and knowing.

When I am here, people notice my accent and ask me where I'm from. The funny thing is, in the other place where I live, where the sound of my voice does not rub rough against a listener's ear, in the place where I keep my books and my cat, I get asked where I'm from too. For as long as I can remember, people have asked me where I'm from.

Perhaps I project some sort of homelessness. Maybe my eyes tell my truth: no matter where I go, I keep myself both inside and outside of things.

In Cape Town, no one expects anything from me and I can slip often into the poetic space of not-knowing. I live here soaked in and confronted by my privileges and labels. I am student, tourist, woman, white, outsider, american, consumer, voyeur, friend, participant, teacher, activist, educated, connected, alone.

Something in this place both accepts and excludes me, again and again like ocean currents that pull me in and push me out. I will never be allowed to say this place is mine or that I belong here. It is this way. I accept it and perhaps I find some comfort in the distance.

It is this distance, this dissonance, that permits a poem to find itself.

Melissa Butler
May 2010, Cape Town

Contents

How things are

Lift the bowl
from the bottom shelf
and hold it

in both hands. Cup
the bowl. Let your palms
feel its weight. Wonder

what has been held
inside it, what it knows
about liquids, solids, creamy

or old. Listen:
your skin soft
against its curved edge. And you remember

your grandmother's table,
a just-ironed piece of linen over its surface.
You place your palms flat,

feel the warmth, touch
your grandmother, learn
something about her hands,

the way they work. And
this is how things are. The touch
and the years

and the wanting
something. You didn't know then
what you know now

and you don't know now
what you knew then. And this too

is how things are.

Leaving

When she needs to leave,
she goes.

Not like the wind
or anything like that.
More like an unraveling
of thread on a tweed coat,
slowly over time
almost unnoticed.

Even she does not notice
when she goes, only realizes
when she finds herself
someplace else. When her feet
touch a ground unfamiliar,
when the air becomes oblique
against her breath.

Only then does she sit on a chair
or a bench to unwind
the path of her leaving,
to discover when
she must have felt the edge
that let her drift away.

From what I know about spiders

At the time I believed it. That it was a meant-to-be kind of love.
And I'm not writing about the love part. I am wondering about the
believing. I can't tell when to make up stories or when to reject all
meaning. It doesn't seem to matter either way.

Spiders don't think about what things mean. They just keep spinning
webs. Yesterday I went to the forest to watch the tree tops mingle
with the sky. I saw a giant web extended between two of the tallest
trees. There was a black object in the center. When the clouds came
by, I could only see the object. When they drifted on, I could see the
web again. I let time pass in this way for hours until my mind spun
itself back to the ground.

I want to know something about the spider who made that web.
Is that her most perfect one? Does she want to live in it forever?
Would she have any sense of loss if she came home to find it washed
away? From what I know about spiders, I am guessing she wouldn't.
She would recognize her web was gone and, out of something close
to habit, she'd spin another.

I wonder what that something-close-to-habit feels like. Maybe it's like
how we find our balance inside a place of gravity, how we know when
we fall and then we get up. I don't think making meaning is like this,
but maybe I can imagine it this way. Maybe if I made meanings like a
spider spins webs it wouldn't hurt so much when I lose them. I could
come home to find everything I know washed away and all I would
have to do is tell another story.

Thinking about edges

An edge allows you to point and say:
Here it is. This is where it begins.
This is where it ends—

the place where something else
happens. An edge of a wall. The edge
of your arm. Edge of sky meets
an edge of sea. This edge of sea
forms an edge of shore that changes
and is not steady as an edge of a table.

An edge of shore sinks down to the bottom
of what some people have given a name
such as Arctic Ocean or Mediterranean.
And there are edges here too.

I have been to the point where the Indian Ocean
meets the Atlantic but I couldn't see the edge.
Couldn't touch it like the edge of my door
as I leave my home or the edge of a page
when I hold my book.

Maybe the currents of the sea
with their changes in temperature and direction
perform a sensory separation of place,
some felt definition between two things.
And perhaps this is similar
to what I feel now

inside this movement of lines
pulling into me and out again——
this stir into emptiness
that drifts between your eyes
and the story I will tell.

Defining distance

The distance between two points
depends upon the location

of the points: how close
together they are, if either moves

farther away from the other,
if something pushes one

in a particular direction. But
there will always be a distance

between two points; otherwise
there would only be one point.

And with one point,
there could be no segment of line,

no section of what goes on forever,
nothing which allows the mind

to travel back and forth between
dreams or glances, disappointment

or the touching of hands. Because
it is, in fact, this space between

two points—what waxes
and wanes as the moon—

that defines each point
where it is

for however long it stays
in a piece of time

that is both eternity
and shadow.

Not so much a lesson, but—

When you lift a shell from where it rests on the sand. When you lift
that shell to hold it for a moment. Feel its curve. Glimpse its present
texture. Lick its salt. When you lift that shell. Even if you put it back
close to the place where you found it. Even if you put it back only a
millimeter closer to the equator or the Southern Pole. Even if you hold
it only for the tiniest speck of what we have come to call time. Even if
you whisper your name onto its surface. Or hold your breath against
its story. You alter that shell's shape forever. Nudge its release of sand
from what it otherwise would be. What it would take from its tides.
You shift its path to another layer, another time. Another fraction of
space that is both here now and was here then. And you become part
of it. Part of its path, part of it all. You are tied to its imprint upon the
earth. Because you bent over to lift it from the place where you found
it. That place next to millions of other places only a footstep from
where you now stand.

No honey

You will know it when you see it:
Your house with the red door
resting against the hillside
or that cloud more perfect
than a baby's eyes. You will know it
in the pit of your stomach
like you knew when you first heard her laugh,
saw her turn her head.

And it sometimes works this way:
You look up and see two Southern Right Whales,
their tails wrapped in a dance
that tugs your heart into the sea.

But sometimes
you turn the corner
a moment before she was there or the wind blows
your hat to the other side of the road
or the elevator rests too long on the third floor.

I can't wrap every story with a bow.
The sky tells me nothing today.

Sometimes it is best to have rooibos
with no honey.

The depth of things

His hand palms the bottom of his glass, transfers heat into the
body of what promises to erupt with textured oak, chocolate, a hint
of blackberry. But his eyes are not patient. (He could not have made
such a wine.) He demands, expects, does not trust what is gentle.
And so I do not like him. I know this is not fair. I should not judge
someone because of his eyes, how he looks at his glass. Should not
size his worldview in a glance. But I do. I am like this. Details matter.
They tell the depth of things. So, I am sad for that wine. For those
grapes. Even for that glass that holds their story.

Urban safari

We went emo spotting today. Walking Long Street in gazes. Looking
for jeans tight, low and hugged as gloves at the ankles. We walked to
catch a glimpse of something other than ourselves, to find an emotional
aesthetic of slippered feet, precise bed-head, a thinness usually reserved
for poles and twigs, sunglasses that eclipse the face. We went to hunt
as anthropological voyeurs without a research question, without a
purpose beyond that of viewing prey, identifying legs, hair, feet. And
then, satisfied with what we found, sat down for a cup of coffee with
the pigeons.

Cited

Everyone[1] loves[2] the[3] mountain.[4] Yet[5] it[6] doesn't[7] strike[8] his[9] heart[10] like[11] the[12] poems[13] say[14] it[15] should.[16]

---

[1] You are included

[2] to enjoy, feel great passion and smile the daydreams of climbing, photography, picnics in the sun—

[3] this particular one of each and every day, the one people reference for the weather, the one on postcards, the one you came to see,

[4] hard table of rock anchored next to fleeting clouds en route to other places.

[5] Otherwise

[6] that which embodies something that might be touched

[7] does not, will not, should not, could not, will never

[8] rupture of a kind of depth that holds

[9] some person perhaps not unlike yourself.

[10] Tracing memory as a finger to palm

[11] is similar to

[12] something known or held as if of earth

[13] in the spaces with holes for minds to fill; dances not yet danced.

[14] Utter

[15] what might be pronounced as a moment next to sea—

[16] ought to be, like a dream or breath coming home.

At a red light

The road. The car. The car on the road. The car on the left side of
the road. The man on the road. The man with his pile of papers for
sale. The man with his pile of papers for sale on the road. The woman.
The woman with a smooth black skirt to her knees and soft shoes.
The woman on the road. She walks somewhere. And the plastic bag.
The plastic bag in a tuft of wiry grass. The plastic bag in the tuft next
to the green pole with almost no more green. The plastic bag in the
tuft of grass by the road. The wind. The wind on the road. The wind
moves a piece of the plastic of the bag. The edge wrinkles, sinks in
slightly, and a blade of the wiry tuft says something. What it says is
not of bags or plastic or tufts or poles. Not of the news of papers or
of women walking. The wrinkle bends almost to a full crease and a
point of the wiry blade pokes through the plastic and holds on. The
blade of grass in the tuft next to the pole next to the road holds onto
the bag, the plastic bag that might otherwise blow away.

Shame

i.
He says it is better
than it was. And
he is good to his staff.
They get paid pretty well.

ii.
There exists a rhythm
of many drums
from the bus station
in the morning.
You can see it too. Like
a tide washing into the city.

iii.
She says she has a right
to keep her bag
on the front seat.
It is her country too.

iv.
There are many things
to buy here: goblets
of etched glass,
carrot cake,
leather shoes with pointed toes,
mango strips, mosaic tables
for the veranda, elaborate
gates to keep the view.

\

Removed (but) still there

I will put 600   (parentheses)
around
the word culture—

              (unbind) it by fluttering

its edges.

     No   (heritage) too tight.

No   custom(s)
overdone.

Nothing authentic   (woven)
into a scarf

              (or) rug
or hat to be   (packaged)
as a gift.

    A gift   (for) you
from here.

Here away   from (there).

You act   (as) witness
to your
own   (postcards).

The name of foreigner

May 2008

We stand around a table to peel potatoes.
Four Muslim South Africans, an Israeli,
a Canadian, an American. We do not talk
about where we're from.
The older women teach us
how to hold the potato, the knife,
how to pull pressure down
gently towards the thumb.
We fill large buckets with what we've carved.

We drive in caravan to Solomon Mahlangu
on the outskirts of Khayelitsha
to deliver crates of bread and a pot of soup
that takes two men to carry.
We drive slowly and think about what it means
to leave a home for another place, who gets
the name of foreigner in a place of need.

She sits on a blue plastic chair,
her baby wrapped to her back
with an orange towel. She waits to be served
four slices of white bread and a Styrofoam cup
of split-pea soup. She speaks from a place
of effort I do not know and says:
Thank you for bringing us food.

The children still smile. To them
it is just another place to explore.
They pick up five-cent coins, pieces of plastic,
small rocks and discarded chicken bones.
They hold pieces of bread folded
in their hands. Take bites and leave crumbs.
When I say: one, two… they say:
three, four, five.

I think about things

Like how in five and a half days I get to have a bubble bath. And
how this rooster slants his neck always to the same side when he
ka-ka-doodles his call. How a topple of ants devoured the slug I
loved this morning. No sky here is ever the same as another. My
raincoat will not be clean again. I will never crave white bread or
white rice or potatoes. But the kingfisher—I will long to watch
him with his dance of hover and dive. And those yellow birds in
the morning who float down as a cloth to sponge the earth. And
how when you sit on a bench you are sitting where story after story
sat before you. On that very same spot. And how if you look at your
hands closely enough you can see everything you have ever touched,
held, embraced, released—a reel of imprints and before-times will
pass into you as a web coming home. And how the ocean roar sounds
like a crowded distant highway leading somewhere beyond what I
imagine, what my mind can wrap itself around. There are so many
types of moths I never knew, ones that look like flower petals or with
a texture of fine tapestry. And I can be surprised by the faintest of
frogs the size of my thumbnail peeking from behind my teacup. I
made my tea from water I did not carry myself. Fiction and fact are
shades of the same—same moment, same memory. Sometimes I feel
my mind carve a memory like sand imprints stone. I wonder if stone
can feel the tickle.

-Tshani Village, Eastern Cape

Whimsy with dirty birds

Today I tried to hate a pigeon. I scowled at it. I called it a name: *ugly, useless, flying rat*. I let my mind imagine it knocked out by a piece of falling concrete at the construction site where it was perched. When it moved its neck like it was doing a little dance, I didn't find it cute. When the morning sun lifted shimmers of lilac and honey from its feathers, I rejected any bit of beauty. When it made that sound pigeons make, I was disgusted at the lack of tone quality, bored by the obvious beat. I did not wonder what it was thinking or daydream about where it might go next. I was working hard to hate that pigeon. *I hate you, I hate you, you silly bird*. I muttered this out loud and people around me thought I was fierce. When the pigeon cocked its head and rotated an eye towards me, I did not fall for its charm. I met that crafty eye with a grimace. I was a hater. No longer will I engage in whimsy with dirty birds. And when that god-damned pigeon finally flew away, I did not watch it go with any longing, nor did I admire its drift of shadow upon the table where I sat. No way will the echo of its exiting flutter remain forever in my heart.

If

Imagine yourself as a fly.
You see quickly
in multiple frames. Now grab
on to a piece of light. You go.
You go fast. You are traveling

fast and seeing fast.
And so everything
looks slow. So slow
it's as if nothing
is happening at all or maybe

it's like everything
has already happened
(it's hard to say the difference).
But there you are—going on
and on like this. I wonder

what you're thinking about. I wonder
what matters to you. And I wonder
what would matter to me
if I could see as fast as a fly
and travel at the speed of light.

Perhaps everything would seem
much the same as now. Or maybe
I would think about how an elephant sees
the world or how it would feel to travel
at the pace of a new dung beetle.

Ritual lines

I.

Their house was lined with shelves.
He insisted that half of them be empty at all times.
Objects could be shifted from shelf to shelf or wall to wall, but

there was always to be equal space between empty and full.
New books, clay bowls, glass sculptures were to be placed
in the entry cupboard to the right of the doorway.

Objects could be traded from the entry cupboard to the shelves
at any time between sunrise and sunset.
Discarded objects (for trade or gift or donation)

were to be placed in the exit drawer under the front closet mirror.
Every twenty-one days he would do a sketch
of the positive and negative space of their shelved home.

Each year on their anniversary
he would hang his sketches along the wall in his study
and as the evening sun brought orange light into the room,

they would sit side-by-side on the carpeted ottoman
to gaze at their lines made from patterns of empty.

II.

She had a game of her own. She would collect lost objects
during her morning walks on the mountain: buttons,
feathers, plastic wrappers, pieces of thread.

When she returned home she would put them in the wooden box
to the left of their door. In the evenings when he was in his study
she would hide her daily treasures

inside the objects on their shelves: between pages in books,
inside clay pots, underneath glass sculptures.
She kept a record of each object's home

in a small yellow notebook. When an object's home got moved,
she would draw a map. When they sat together every year
to gaze at his sketches of their shelves,

she would thread stories from object to object
that only she could see.

Sacred

This day stands still.

There is no wind
and I have nothing to say.

There is breath;
even memories rise and fall.

Some things exist more
when we cannot see them.

We make it this way
to lift away the heavy,
dissolve the order,

so we can hold ourselves
in place.

To believe is to tell a story,
find prayer
inside a labyrinth.

There is the story of the ibis,
the sacred one
who flies from sky to sea
to forage in clumps of kelp,

the one who brings light as Thoth——
mind of god——the one who knows,

who comes each day
without a sound.

What gathers slowly

If this city has become
any other city and your life is
any other life,

maps and clocks are not to blame.

There is a rhythm that builds
from the familiar,
gathers itself slowly
as measured time
held in a locket.

(In a whisper):
Do not hold what is precious.

I am telling you this
because all things
will return to sand.

This is why I trust glass blowers:
they know about the breaking.

And that day,
the one that made you feel
like nothing else mattered, the one
that made you say *everything
is alright now,* that day,

even that day is gone.

(Remember): The familiar
gathers itself slowly
and then you are there, in a life edged
by dinner time, a garbage truck
and the neighbor
who walks her dog.

And this is why infinity matters:

So I can find layers inside
the details; lifetimes

I will never hold.

Of searching

And what of the frog who perches all day in the same spot.
Or the kettle that does not whistle. The crease
that will not remain flat. Or the bird
battling the wind.

And what of her reach across the table to take
what she needs. His eyes grazing the angle
of her neck. The faint music from her spoon
around the inside of her cup
that only he hears.

And what of her dream. Of the slug on a wall
of faint shadow and slime. Of her car
without wheels. Of the cupboard that empties itself
when she opens it. Shelves no longer
even with dust.

And what of this thing she feels outside
of what she knows. Outside of time
and the order of days. This thing that grabs into her
but takes nothing.
Only stirs her awake.

And what of the days with their rises and sets.
With their three o'clock appointments
and dinner guests. With buzzes to come in
and robots red.

And what of the road that ends somewhere. Stops
when it must because of mountain or sea.
In this space of edges, of layered time
we touch but cannot see. After all,
this is where we are.

This

Today I can't tell
the sky from the shore;
the heavy white
blurs the ground.
I blend into the scene
on the road.

My mind holds
only the small things
today; I rest
on the cusp of silence,
but am not quite still.

Tree branches are
the mirror of their roots.

I believe this today
because my heart
needs a pocket.

I can't say it softer
than this: I need you
to find me

and bring me home.

Hadeda geographies

Hadedas are nothing much to notice
until you hear them—*haa haa dee dah*.
Some consider them a nuisance
that interrupts morning love-making
or evening conversations on the veranda,
but for others their call echoes home.
It is often said they call for the rain
or call about it coming. I think
they might be saying something else.

Southern Right Whales come each winter
to breed—swim in playful circles
close to shore. Their large flukes sailing
with the wind, rough white patches
on their heads. People travel great distances
for boat rides and coastal hikes
that bring them closer:
close enough to hear
what these ancient beings have to say.

The dassie is a small rodent-like creature
who lives in mountain rocks and trees
near the sea. It is the closest living relative
to the elephant. I love that someone
figured this out: noticed similarities
between tusks and incisors, studied
pads on soles of feet, traced
the abdominal placement of testes
to a large, distant relative.

Stories seem to evolve with animals:
How leopard got so many spots, why
crocodile has big teeth, the reason
crow sings inside a full moon. But stories
are not only for children. We need them
to tell us what things mean.
So we know what matters
and when to let go.

People migrate to the city each day—
a tide of uniformed blue washing in
with the first glimpse of light
and washing out as the sun casts
deep orange low on the horizon.
The circadian of the city. Every day,
except Sundays, this happens. People come
and go in a rumble of earth—a pulse
that remains after they have moved on.

Hadedas travel almost the same route
every day. They are punctual to and from
their feedings—*haa haa dee dah*.
They are as predictable as morning coffee
or late afternoon tea. Their rhythms
follow the moon. They come and go
underneath a scumbled sky
pushing sea against sea.

Mollusks begin as larvae,
then attach their mantles
to fish hosts for nutrients
that grant them freedom to leave,
to move on to other places: boulders,
fishing boats, whales.
Some of these places travel;
others stand still. I wonder
if mollusks can tell the difference.

Animals get clues to tell them
when to move; they follow sun or stars,
scent, magnetic field, memory. They go
in search of water or food, a better climate.
They go where they go to get what they need.
Some movement is grand: wildebeest
in tides across the Serengeti. Others travel
outside our view: a blanket of moths
in a night sky or a lone sea turtle mother
seeking land to lay her eggs.

Touch sends signals
from the bottom layer of skin
through the spinal cord to the brain.
This path registers the feeling,
tells us where we are,
that there is something to know.

Bees go into and out of petals
to collect what they need.
A metronome of wings in pursuit
of what tastes sweet, what nourishes larvae,
what might become honey.
Some bees go home at night,
but others stay to drift asleep
inside the hold of a flower.

Hadedas fly to the ground
in pairs—*haa haa dee dah*.
They land in cattle kraals and open fields
to probe the earth
with long downward curved bills.
They eat earthworms and insects, spiders
and snails. They feed by what they feel.
They feel to feed.

What begins as mountain or hillside
eventually turns to sand.
Time moves in this way. But dreams
are a different kind of time.
They work in labyrinths
to send glimpses we cannot count.
Dreams open what we hold in our skin:
footsteps, salt, stories.

Galaxies hold solar systems and solar systems
hold stars, planets, asteroids and moons.
There are billions of galaxies layered in this way.
Everything is where it is
because of the push and pull of things
in relation to their mass.
This is all we are:
matter in constant tug with other matter,
trying to hold on to our place.

Some creatures build their homes
out of habit: beavers, ants, spiders, birds.
If something comes along to destroy the place
where they live, to sweep it away or step on it,
if it gets dismantled by weather or human hands,
what happens is this: they build it again;
collect branches or twigs, haul pieces of sand,
find another place to begin.

Male baboons stay with a troop only
for so long before they leave to disperse
themselves in a Southerly,
in search of another place.
Every so often a baboon does not find his way
to a new troop and so he stays alone.
Some people think this is sad,
but it is the way of things.

Hadedas do not perch, but they do come home.
It is here where they nest and do their billing—
intertwine necks and preen each other.
They grasp bills and rattle:
move their heads up and down, side to side.
This is how they ask each other to stay.
This is how they tell each other what matters:
touch, sky, holding on—*haa haa dee dah*.

I want to know how to find my way home.
Not by sight or sound
or following a map. I want to feel it
without my mind tackling it down.
Know it like the hadedas know
when to leave and when to stay.

I want to feel this kind of knowing:
how it threads its way through me, how it
pulls me in, where it shows me to go.
I want to know from a place
outside of what we know about knowing,
away from dream or memory;
somewhere inside instincts of skin.

I want to know what the spiders know,
what the sea turtles tell their young,
what moths want from the wind.
I want to feel movement across fields,
the tug of magnetism against my breath.
I want the urgency of it all: the need to take,
to go, to come back.

I want to hold what cannot be known,
fold it into me, let it stay. And then maybe
I will find what the hadedas have to say:
what they call for, what they want from us,
what they know about knowing
and letting go——*haa haa dee dah.*

Acknowledgements

This book would not have been possible without sabbatical/study leave from the Pittsburgh Public Schools and the support of all my teacher friends in the Western PA Writing Project. In SA, many people have nurtured my writing and for this, I am most grateful. A special thanks to Martha Evans, Neo Muyanga, Kathryn Nurse, Tania van Schalkwyk, Liz Trew, Finuala Dowling, Femi Terry and Colleen Higgs. And a big thank you to my advisor, Stephen Watson.